FRANZ BRANDENBERG

THE HIT OF THE PARTY

Pictures by ALIKI

THE BODLEY HEAD
LONDON

British Library Cataloguing in Publication Data
Brandenberg, Franz
The hit of the party.
Rn: Aliki Brandenberg   I. Title   III. Aliki
823 [J] PZ7   ISBN 0-370-30892-1

Text copyright © 1985 by Franz Brandenberg
Illustrations copyright © 1985 by Aliki Brandenberg
All rights reserved. Printed in Great Britain for
The Bodley Head Ltd, 30 Bedford Square, London WC1B 3RP
by Cambus Litho, East Kilbride
*First published by Greenwillow Books, William Morrow & Co. Inc.,
New York, 1985   First published in Great Britain 1985*

For
Ariadne
and
Leon

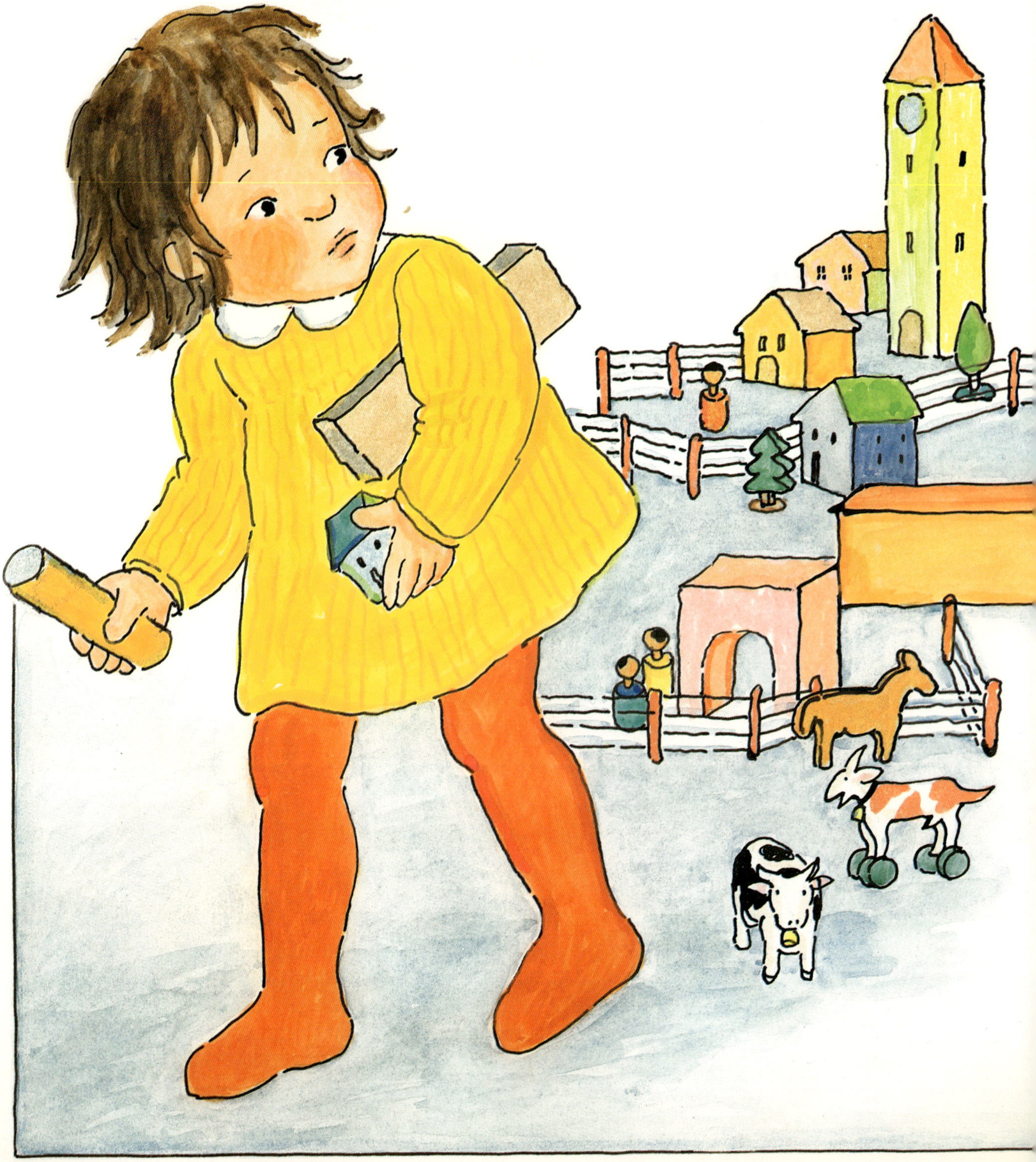

"I am going to be the hit of the party," said Jim.

"So am I," said Kate.

"No, you won't," said Jim.

"I am going to be a rooster, and you are going to be just a hen."

"What's the difference?" asked Kate.
"A rooster has beautiful tail feathers," said Jim. "And a hen doesn't."

"So what!" said Kate. "Anyway, it's time to get dressed for the party."
"I have to feed Cheeks first," said Jim.
"But hurry up!" said Kate.

Jim took the seeds to his hamster's cage.
But it was empty.
"Cheeks has escaped!" shouted Jim.
"Please help me find her!"

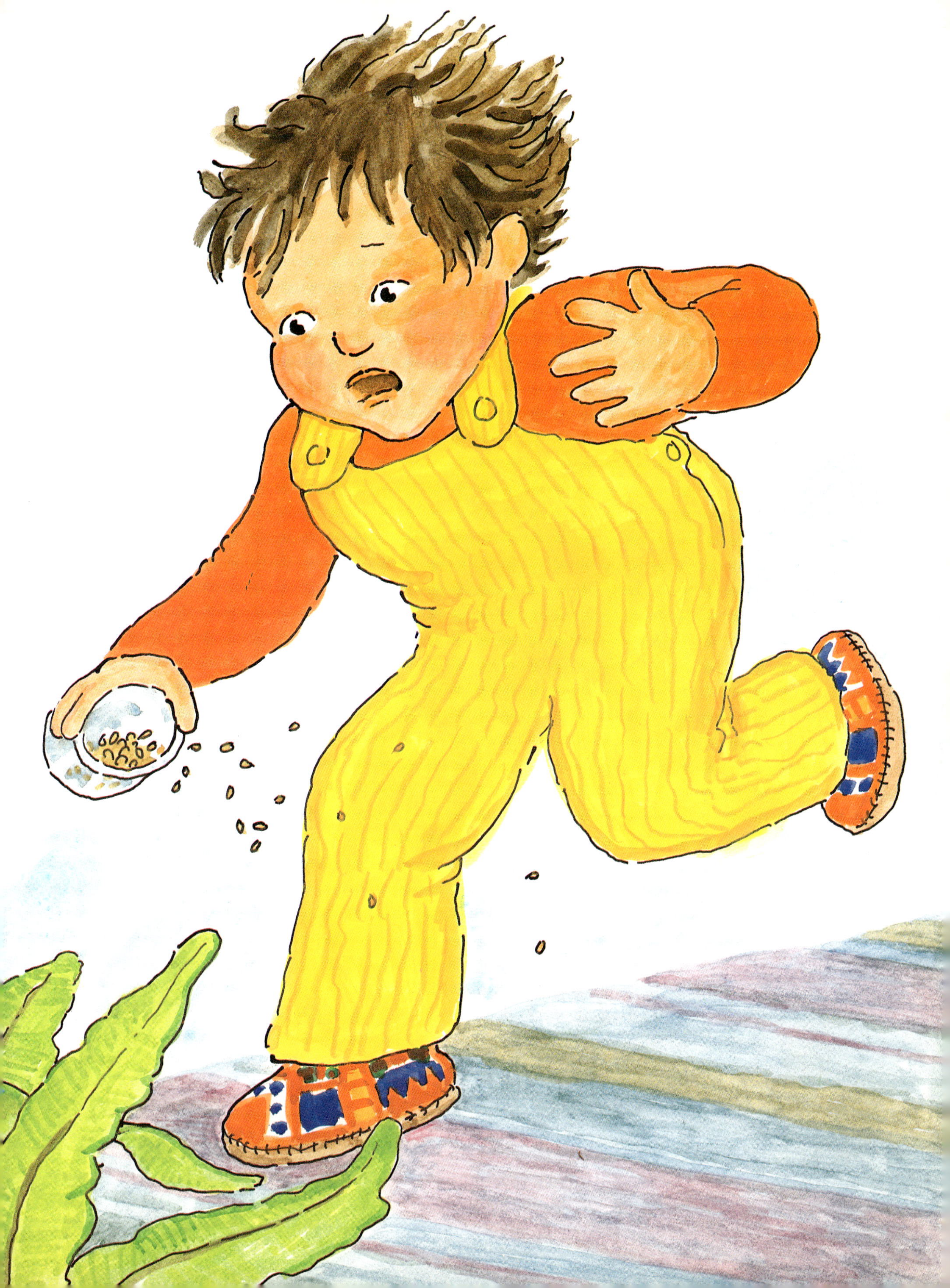

Jim and Kate and their parents searched everywhere.
But they couldn't find Cheeks.

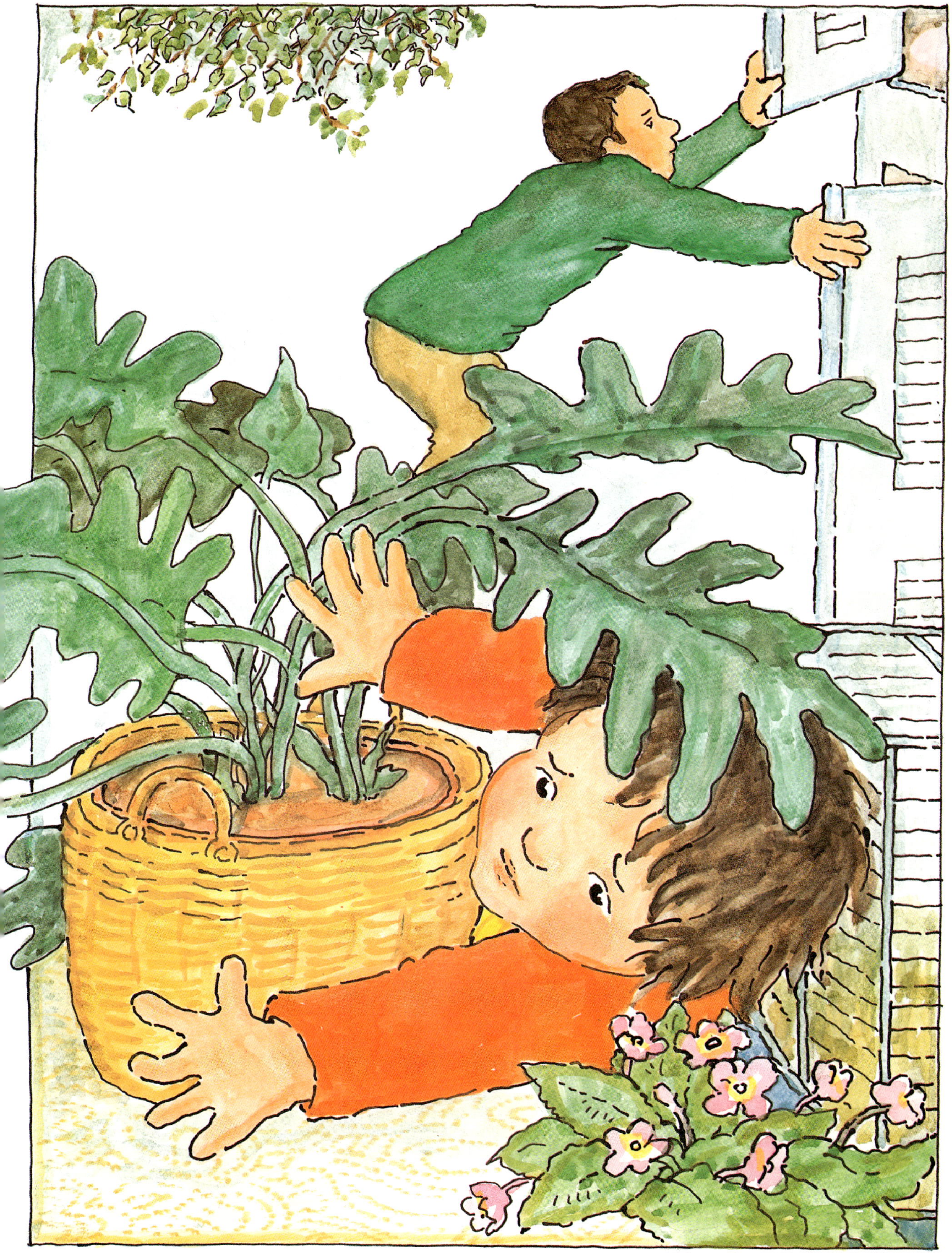

"I have lost her," cried Jim.

"We'll buy you another hamster," said Father.

"I don't want another hamster," said Jim. "I want Cheeks."

"It's almost time for the party," said Mother.

"I don't care," said Jim. "I want Cheeks."

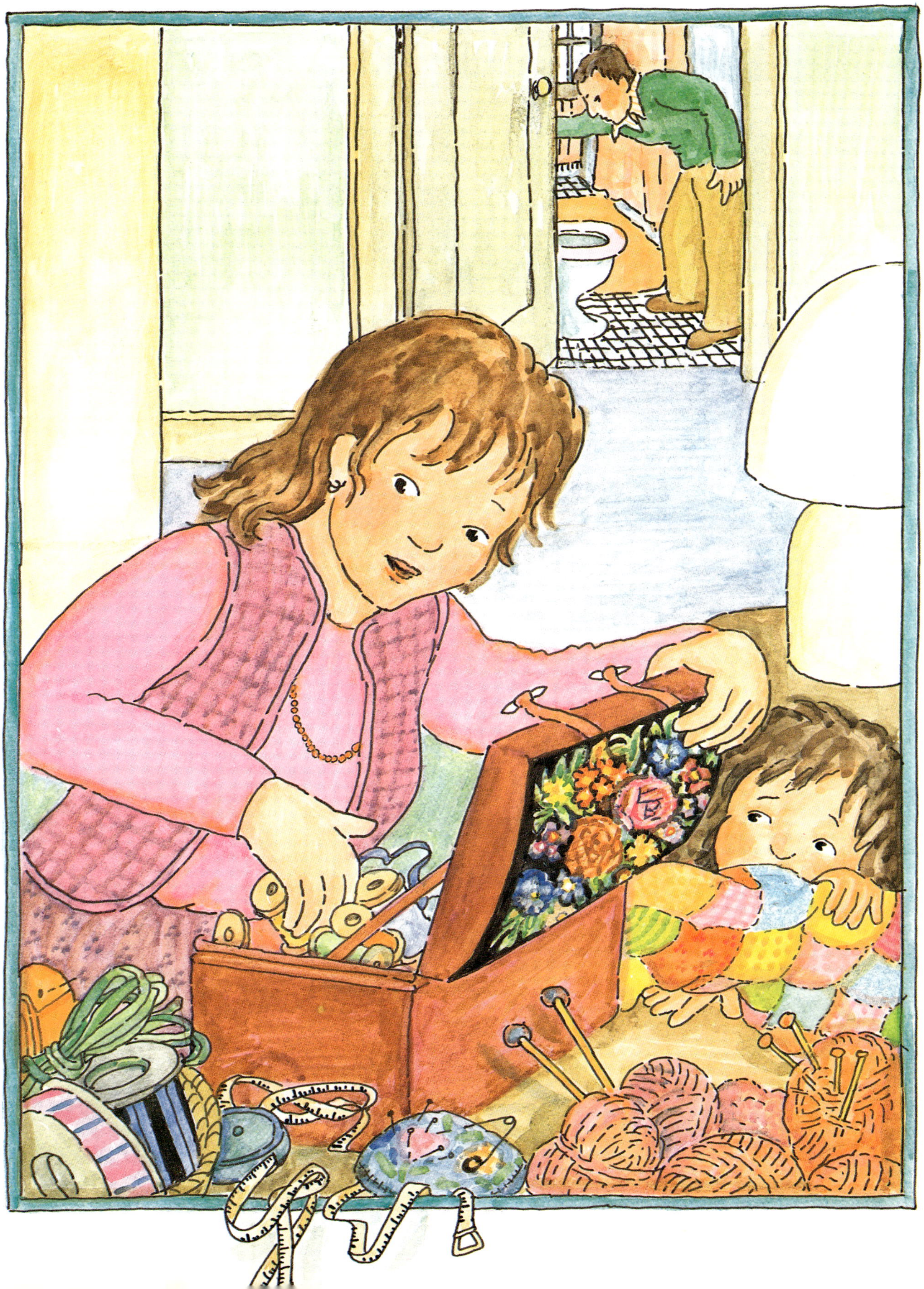

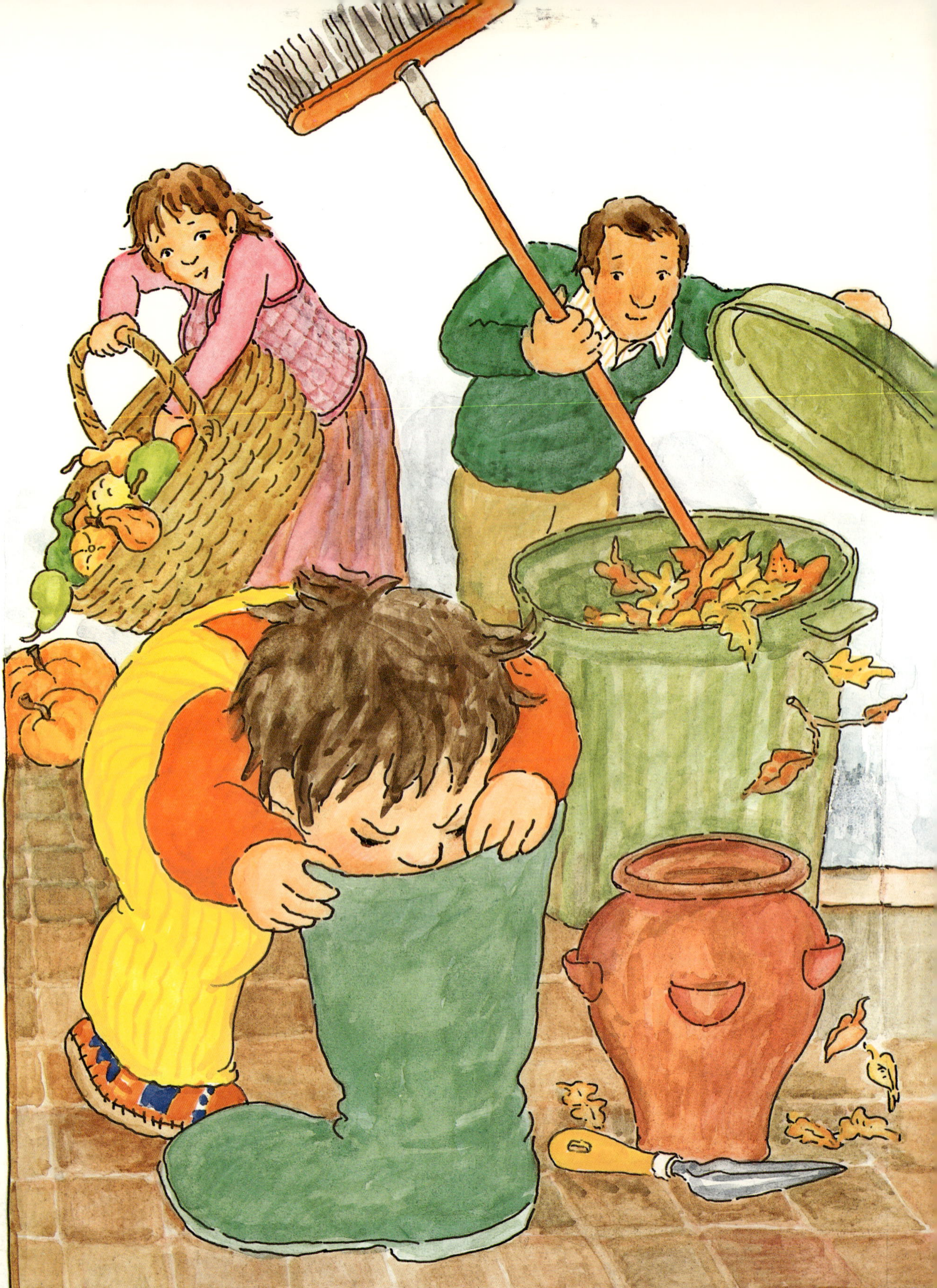

"Your friends will be surprised when they see your costume," said Father.

"I don't care," said Jim. "I want Cheeks."

"You are going to be the biggest rooster ever," said Mother.

"I don't care," said Jim. "I want Cheeks."

"We'll miss the party if we don't go soon," said Kate.

AUGUST
1 2 3 4 5 6 7 8 9 10 11 12 13 14 15
16 17 18 19 20 21 22 23 24 25 26 27
28 29 30 31

Jim went to his cupboard.

He took out his costume.

"Oh, no!" he cried. "Look what you have done!"

"I haven't done anything," said Kate.

"You cut off my tail feathers," said Jim.

"I did not!" said Kate.

"You tore them into bits," said Jim.

"I did not!" said Kate.

"Look at them!" said Jim, pointing to a heap of shredded feathers.

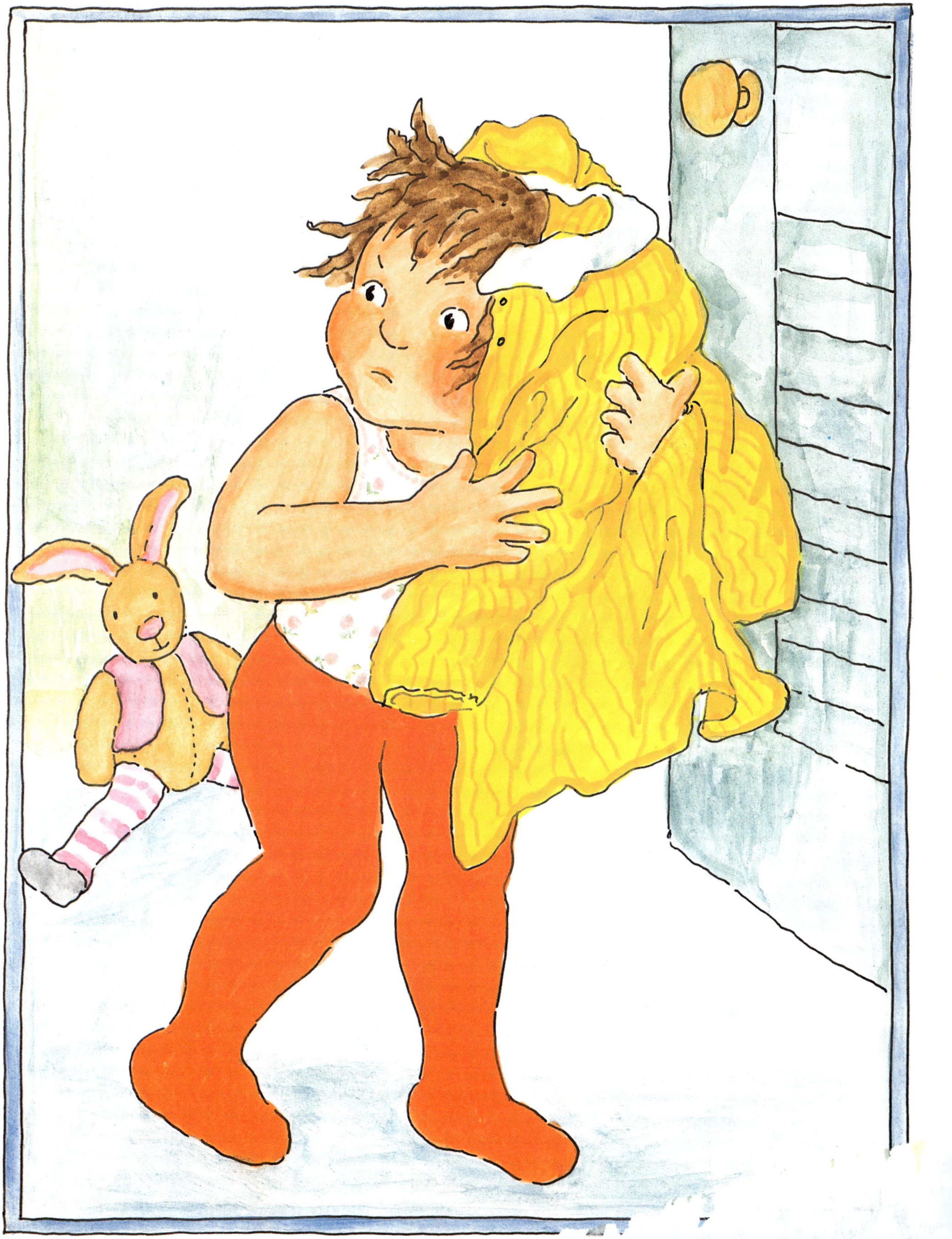

"And there is Cheeks in them!" cried Kate.

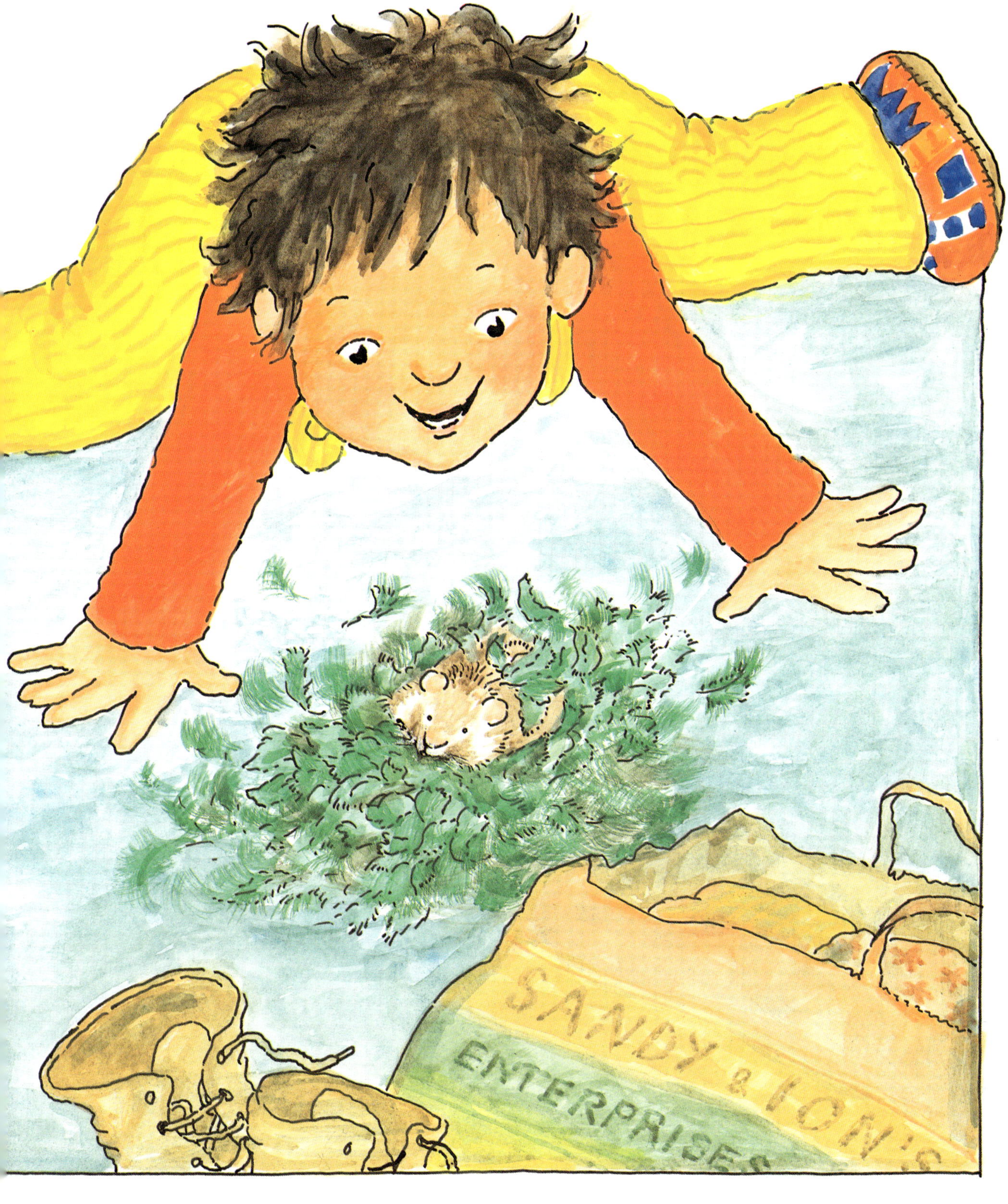
SANDY & ION'S
ENTERPRISES

"She is the one who bit off your feathers,"
said Mother.

"How naughty of her!" said Kate.

"She made herself a nest with them," said Father.

"I don't care about the feathers," said Jim.

"I am so happy I have found Cheeks."
He put his hamster into the cage,
and fed her.

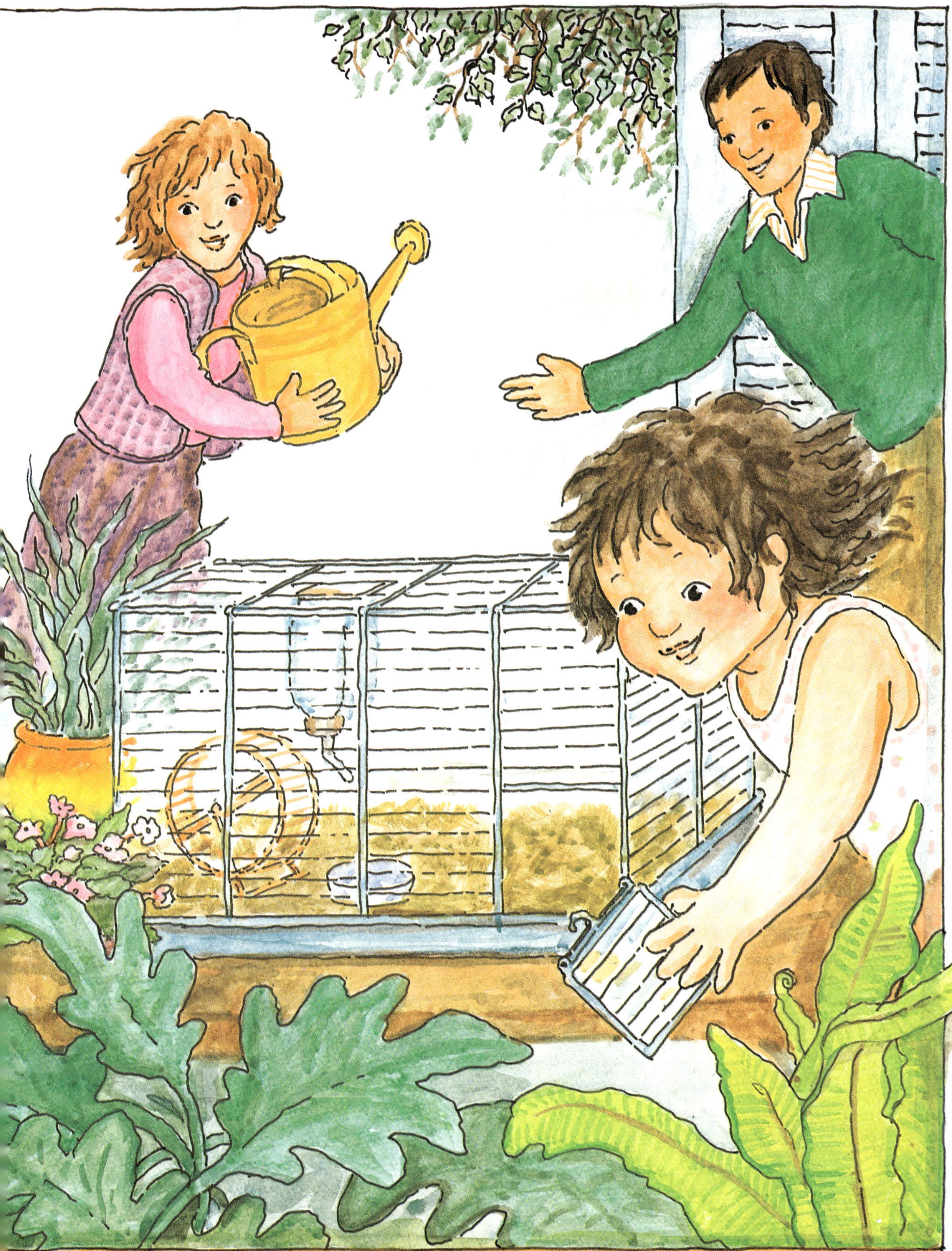

"I guess you don't feel like going to the party now," said Kate.
"Of course, I do," said Jim.
"Now that I have found Cheeks."

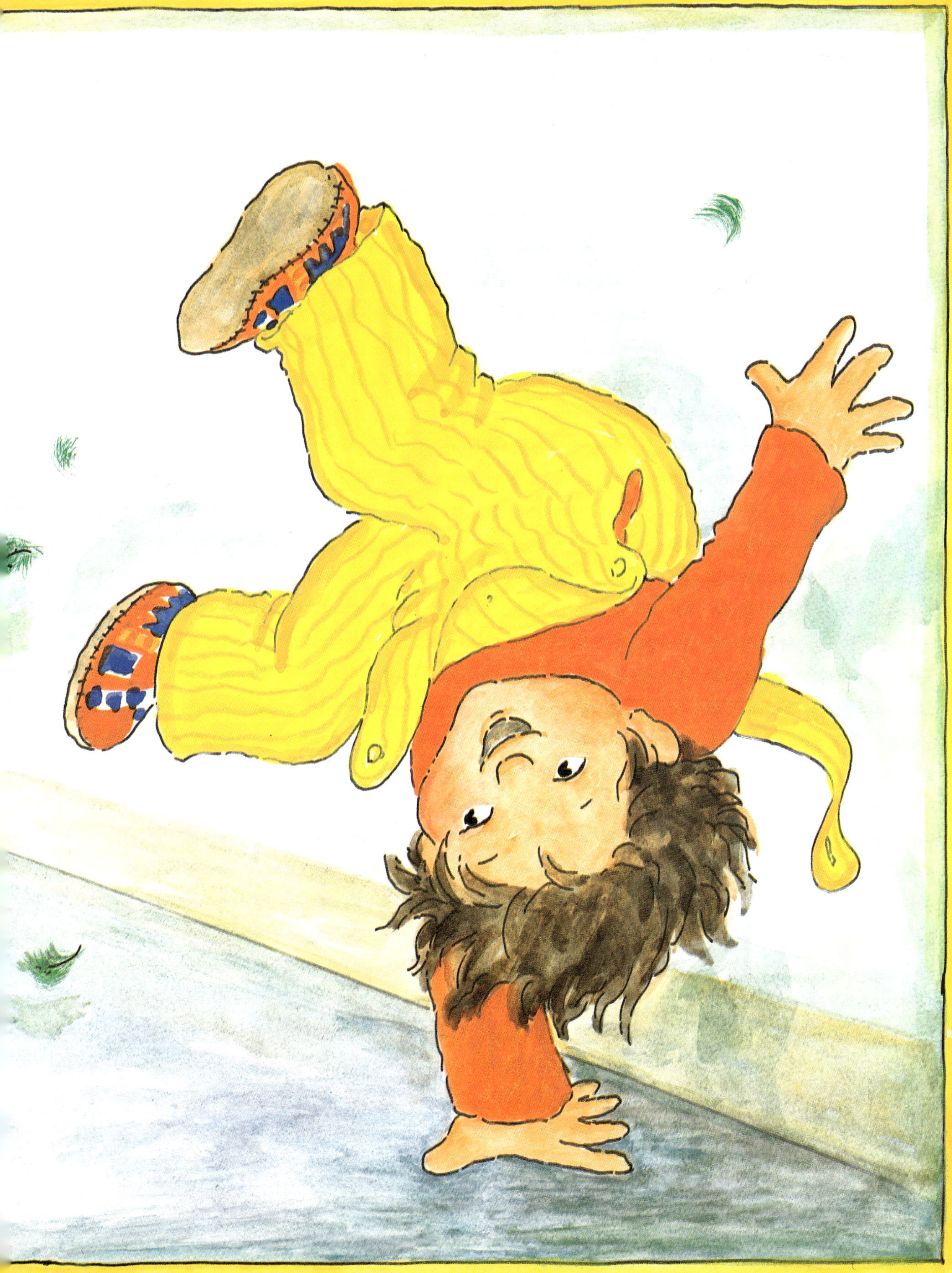

"But you won't be a rooster," said Kate.

"So what!" said Jim.

"We'll be two hens instead."

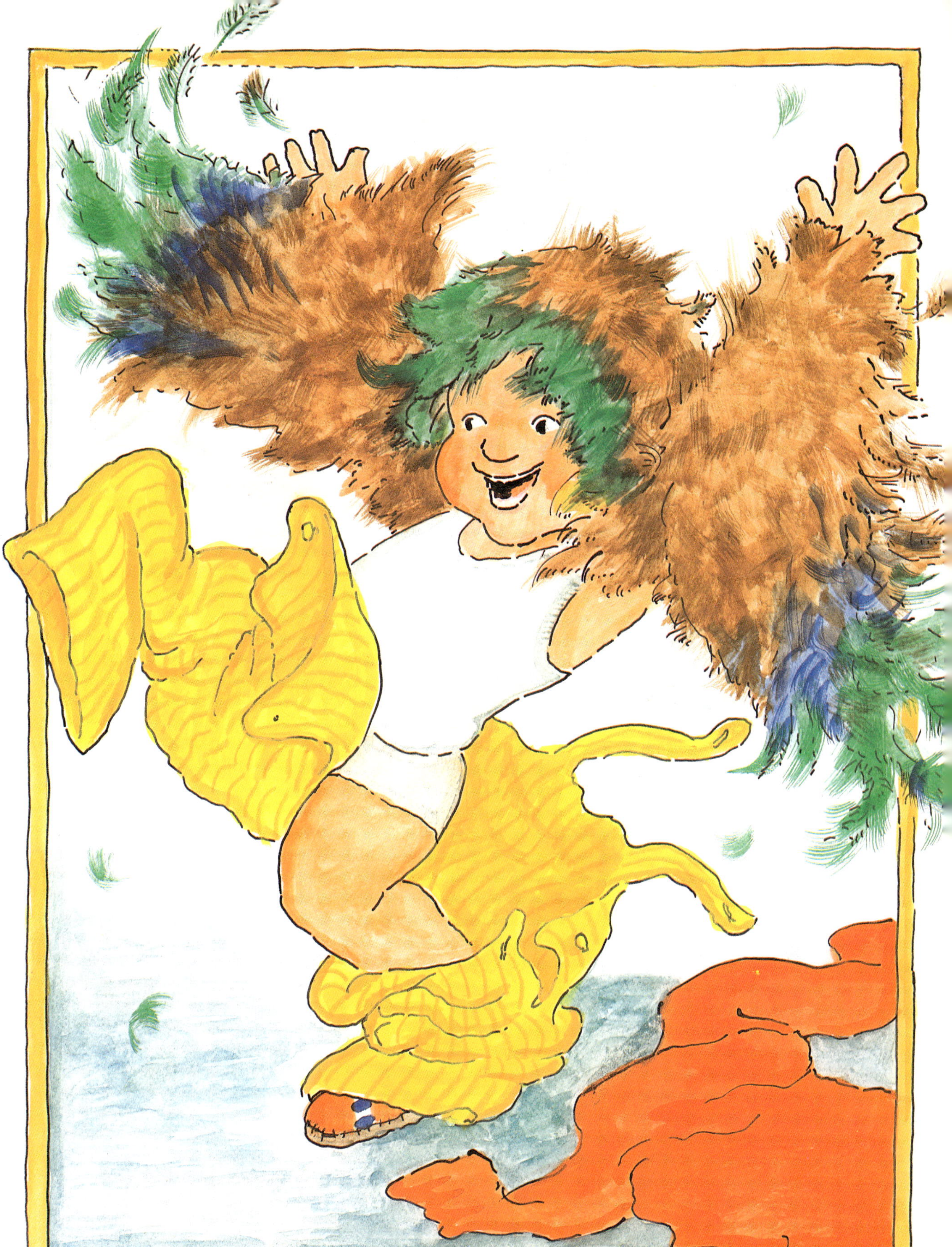

Kate and Jim were the biggest hens ever.

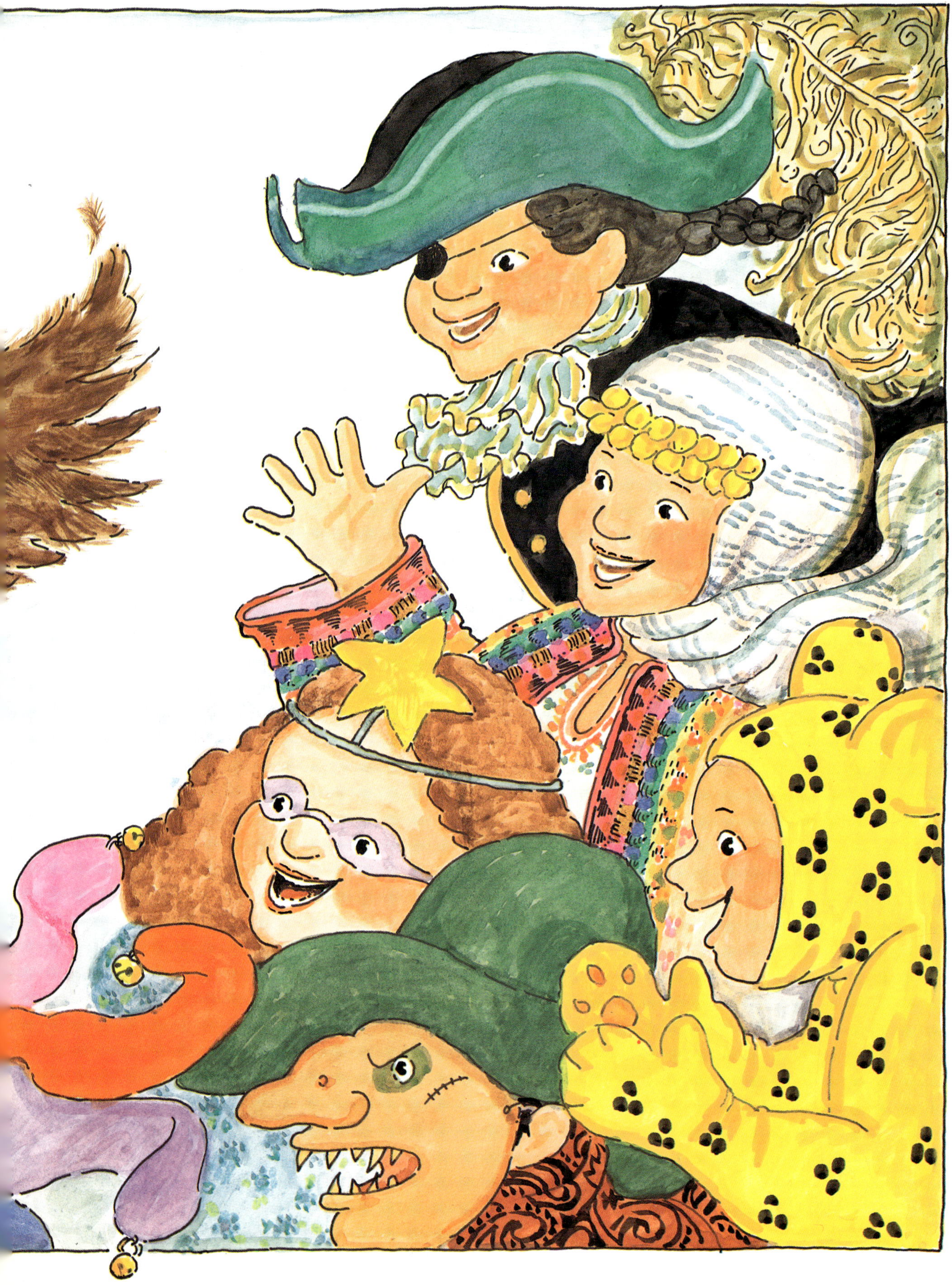

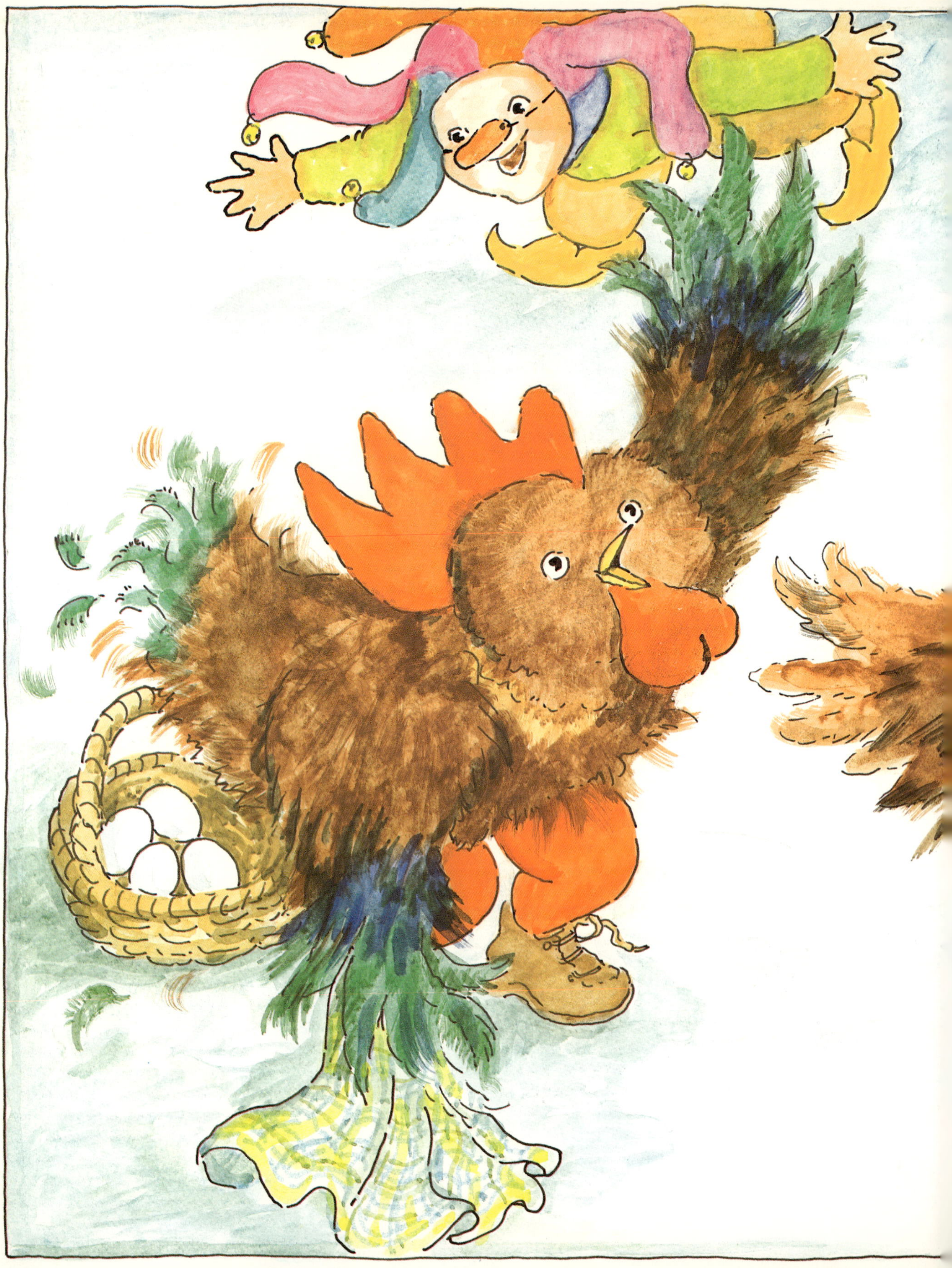

And they both were the hit of the party.